# DELIB ACTS OF
# NE
# MEANNESS

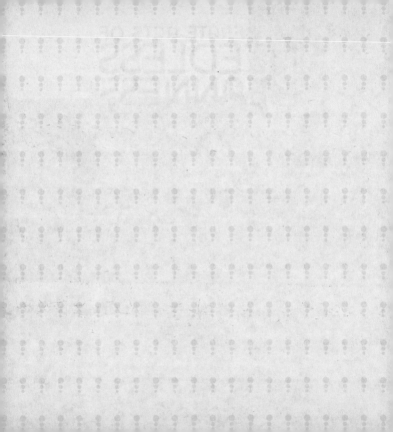

# DELIBERATE ACTS OF
# NEEDLESS
# MEANNESS

## A Miscellany of *Mischief*-Making

by Justin Rosenholtz

RUNNING PRESS

Philadelphia ✳ London

First published in the United States in 2006
by Running Press Book Publishers.
All rights reserved under the Pan-American
and International Copyright Conventions.

Printed in China

9  8  7  6  5  4  3  2  I
Digit on the right indicates the number
of this printing

Library of Congress Control Number:
2005930672

ISBN-13: 978-0-7624-2535-8
ISBN-10: 0-7624-2535-0

This book was conceived, designed,
and produced by
THE IVY PRESS LIMITED
The Old Candlemakers,
Lewes, East Sussex BN7 2NZ, UK

Creative Director  Peter Bridgewater
Gift Publisher  Stephen Paul
Publisher  Sophie Collins
Editorial Director  Jason Hook
Art Director  Karl Shanahan
Senior Project Editor  Caroline Earle
Designer  Nicola Liddiard
Illustrator  Ivan Hissey
Page Makeup  Richard Peters

This book may be ordered by mail
from the publisher. Please include
$2.50 for postage and handling.
But try your bookstore first!

Running Press Book Publishers
125 South Twenty-second Street
Philadelphia, Pennsylvania 19103-4399

Visit us on the web!
**www.runningpress.com**

# CONTENTS

❧

# INTRODUCTION

Of course you're a nice person. We are all nice people. We spend our days doing nice things. A cheery hello to a stranger here, a helpful act there, and sometimes genuinely going out of our way to do a special kindness to someone.

And do you know what? Sometimes it can get pretty tiring. Who really cares if someone's child took their first step? So what if it's your best friend's birthday? Everyone has a stupid birthday and they happen all the time. You know, like every single year. Your parents weren't perfect, so why the hell do you keep calling them? And guess what, maybe your friend has been on a diet for six months, but quite frankly there's no escaping the fact that she still has a big fat ass.

But still, day after day, you chug along, doing all the right things, and being the pleasant person you are. Never acknowledging the anger and bitterness that is welling inside.

Well, this book is a lifesaver for you. It is chock full of ideas to entertain your inner meanie. There are small things you can do that will cause limited amounts of misery and discomfort to people you don't care about. And even if you never actually do them, you can still have the vicarious pleasure of reading this little book and imagining doing them. Just in case you're keen to be mean, but anxious about the consequences, none of this meanness involves vandalism, lawbreaking, or criminal damage being caused to anybody or anything. So at the very least, if you do any of these mean things, you won't end up in jail surrounded by really mean people.

When we were children, we were happily mean to our siblings, our schoolmates, our teachers, and our parents. Oh, what fun we had. Don't you feel nostalgia for those halcyon days? Everyone tells us we should recapture our youth whenever possible. So why not act like a child and spoil parties, insult family members, and have tantrums in front of complete strangers?

Surely there can be nothing wrong with being mean to your ex. After all they broke up with you and they should pay. And is there anything more annoying than a successful friend? With some needless meanness, you can take annoying to a whole new level. Your family is also in for a pranking. Oh, and don't forget all those idiotic strangers one has to deal with every day. Practice a little meanness in the workplace and your company will rue the day they ever hired you.

So go on. Indulge your fantasy. You're a good person at heart. But sometimes, just sometimes, don't you get tired of keeping that devil inside you down? Go on. Let him out. And see just how good a few deliberate acts of needless meanness can make you feel.

# • STRANGERS •

NEVER DEPEND ON THE KINDNESS OF STRANGERS

## SAY CHEESE

When tourists ask you to take their photo, make sure you don't get their heads in the shot. They'll soon stop troubling locals.

# WHAT TICKET?

Is the local traffic cop being a little overzealous? Has he given you one ticket too many? Try parking where you shouldn't, then putting superglue on your windshield wiper, so that when he picks it up to put that ticket under it...

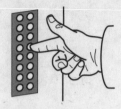

# I BELIEVE IT'S YOUR FLOOR

The next time you're in an empty elevator, press
all the floor buttons just before you get out.

NOTED

Pick a ridiculously oversized four-wheel drive car. Put a note under the windshield wiper that says: "Dear Neighbor, I saw a car hit yours earlier today. A bit of your car fell off, but the other driver stuck it back on again and drove away." Then settle down at a nearby café to watch as they push and pull at every bit of their car.

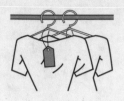

## SIZE ZERO

If overly thin fashionistas annoy you, make sure you visit the clothes shops they haunt, and swap labels so that the clothes are marked two sizes bigger than they actually are. They will think they have put on weight, and become so weak from the extra dieting that they will not have the strength to brag about how thin they are.

## COUNTRY BUMPKIN

If you live in the country, and are sick of city folk taking over your idyllic little town every weekend, adjust the direction signs at junctions so that potential visitors get hopelessly lost. With a bit of luck, they will never come back.

## ON THE SAME PAGE

No book with a bookmark in it should be left without moving the bookmark to a different page. That'll cure the bookworms of their intellectual pretensions and teach them to watch television like normal people.

## COUGH COUGH

Next time you see an unattended shopping cart at the grocery store, slip out a few essential items like milk, butter, and cough medicine. Imagine your victim being kept awake all night by the sound of their own coughing.

# WHO'S YOUR DADDY?

Pick a name out of the telephone directory. Call
and tell whoever answers that you are the child of
the man of the house. Don't hang up until you
hear fighting on the other end of the phone.

## ISN'T HE ADORABLE?

Everyone appreciates a small, screaming child. Be sure you bring an especially loud one on your next airplane journey—even if you have to borrow one from your neighbor.

## BAD HAIR DAY

Print business cards with your name stating: "Attorney. Specializes in Suing Hairdressers." Give these to people with bad hair and tell them you can get them a huge settlement.

# BE POLITE

**:**

Make a move as if you are offering your seat to an older person on a crowded train. When they gratefully say thank you, tell them that if they have enough strength to get on the train, they have enough strength to stand the whole journey.

# EVERY PICTURE TELLS A STORY

Whenever someone troubles you with photos of
the people in their life they are proud of, such
as spouses and children, always proclaim loudly:
"Oh dear. Well, never mind. I'm sure they have
a lovely personality."

## POSTURE PERFECT

Next time you go to a movie be sure to sit up tall—it is healthy for your spine. And if you block the view of the jackass in the seat behind you, well, these things can't be helped.

# EXCUSE ME

As long as you are at the movies, pick a middle seat, and spend the entire movie getting up and going past everyone in your row, saying "excuse me" politely but very loudly. Try to pick your moments, such as when the identity of the murderer is about to be revealed.

## MOVIE STAR

That request for people to switch off their cell phones at the movies does not apply to you. You are far too important. Nobody will mind your frequent incoming calls.

ATCHOO!

:

Have you got an awful cold? Attend a nice healthy yoga class and share it with your classmates. After all, everyone knows you can never truly get rid of a cold until you have given it to someone else.

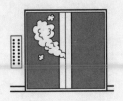

## GAS ATTACK

When next in an empty elevator, fart just before you get out. Enjoy imagining the embarrassed looks of denial being silently exchanged by the next group of people who get in.

# MILE-HIGH CLUB

Take a flight after not bathing for a week. A smelly person in the economy section of a airplane can annoy up to two hundred people simultaneously.

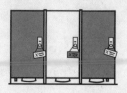

## OUT OF ORDER

Never visit a public restroom without a huge pile of Out of Order signs to put on all the stalls but one. Sit and chuckle as you hear the lines grow long and patience grow short.

## GOOD ADVICE

Next time you see someone alone in a bar who is obviously waiting for a friend who is late, helpfully suggest to them that they have been stood up. Patiently explain that they look like someone who will be alone for the rest of their life.

# WHAT NOT TO WEAR

Go up to a stranger and tell them that while you
don't work for the TV show *What Not To Wear*, you
feel sure that they would be a prime candidate for
it. Offer them an application form to fill out.

# SEVEN DOWN

Many people love their crossword puzzles. That is why you should take every opportunity to take their newspaper while they're not looking, and fill in several clues incorrectly. Write in ink.

# DO YOU HAVE THE TIME?

Whenever someone stops you on the street to ask the time, be sure to make it a half hour earlier than it really is. This will give the stranger a sense they need not hurry to their appointment. As they casually stroll into their meeting they will discover that they are extraordinarily late.

## HELP WANTED

:

If you are nosy and a control freak, why not place an advertisement in the newspaper for a job vacancy that doesn't exist? You can spend an enjoyable day interviewing "candidates," making them feel uncomfortable and untalented, and asking them intrusive questions about their work and private life.

## A TESTING IDEA

!

Volunteer to monitor an exam this summer. Then freak out the unlucky kids by putting a totally different subject's exam questions on selected desks. Give them a good ten minutes of silent torment before you announce that "someone in the office" may have made a mistake, and slowly distribute the correct papers instead.

## NOT SO FRESH

When taking a train be sure to pack some strong-smelling food for a leisurely snack. Tuna fish sandwiches and aromatic Limburger cheese are particularly welcomed by jammed-in commuters on a hot afternoon.

# BREAKDOWN

!

Next time you are driving and you see someone
on the side of the road with car trouble, don't
just drive on. Instead, stop and offer to help. Of
course, roadside "assistance" involves standing
around criticizing and offering incorrect advice.

## SMILE FOR THE CAMERA

•
•
•

Whenever you see a tourist taking a picture of a landmark, always time your walk by to coincide with the click of the camera. If you get good at this trick, the next step is to give a cheery wave when you step into their picture. Eventually you will become a celebrity among photo developers around the world.

## WET PAINT

Make it your life's work to go around removing all the "Wet Paint" signs you encounter. If you think about it, they are usually carelessly lettered, they aren't at all pretty, and they deprive us of the amusing sight of people walking around with paint smudges on their backsides.

## GETTING A BUZZ

•
•
•

Need to spend some time in an enclosed space, like a waiting room or train car? Carry a small tape recorder hidden in your pocket or bag, with a recording of a wasp buzzing. Play it from time to time, and enjoy the increasing fear and paranoia around you. The hours will fly by. The wasp never will.

# THE LAST TRAIN TO CLARKSVILLE

Regularly collect the railway timetables at your local railroad station. When the timetables change, replace the new leaflets with your collection of out-of-date ones. Pop along and sympathize with furious travelers who have missed their last train and don't understand why.

# I AM A SPEED CAMERA

Choose a stretch of road late at night. Position yourself next to a speed camera with your own camera and flash unit. Take flash photographs of only those cars that slow down to beat the speed camera. Enjoy the looks of agony and bewilderment in the resulting snapshots.

## BAD LANGUAGE

Infiltrate a language school for a day. It is vital to send foreign students back to their countries having been taught the wrong words for things. Imagine your pride at seeing one of your ex-students addressing the UN with the words: "I am very horny to be here."

# I WAS ONLY AWAY FOR A MINUTE

•
•

Put an envelope on someone's windshield, so that as they are returning to their car it will look like they have been given a ticket. Imagine their thoughts of indignation as, walking toward their car, they spot the envelope from a distance.

## ALL ROADS LEAD...

If someone asks you for directions and you don't know, just make it up. At least they'll end up somewhere. Think of all those boring people who, when asked for directions, just shrug their shoulders and say, "I don't know."

# ENTENTE UNCORDIALE

•
•

Spend a day being rude in whatever way you choose, but do it with a French accent. When confronted by angry people, say, "I cannot help myself. I'm French." This way, not only do you get to be mean to everyone you meet, but you get to be mean to a WHOLE country.

## CELEBRITY STARES

If you see a celebrity, go up to them and ask for an autograph. After they've signed, look at it and say, sighing with disappointment, "I thought you were someone else."

# THE BUTLER DID IT

As you leave a very popular movie and walk past the line waiting for the next show, be sure to discuss the surprise ending as loudly as you can. The fist-waving may turn out to be more entertaining than the movie itself.

## SCREEN AND SCREEN AGAIN

⦂

The movies are a fun place in which to cause confusion. As you sit waiting for *Death Kill Three* to start, tell the stranger next to you how much you are looking forward to *Women and Lovers*. When they say that this screen is showing *Death Kill Three*, inform them it started next door ten minutes ago. Watch them grab their popcorn and run.

# BURIED TREASURE

At the beach, bury some cans and worthless metal. Then watch all the dreary metal-detector guys get excited because they think they've found something immensely valuable.

## BOOR TASTE

!

When abroad always choose a restaurant that
specializes in the very finest local cuisine.
Ostentatiously reject all of it and then have the
chef prepare a cheeseburger and fries. Loudly
proclaim that the only good food is "back home."
This is also being mean to your own countrymen,
because you will cause everyone to hate them.

# FIVE-STAR COMFORT AT A NO-STAR PRICE

⋮

Have you just stayed in a terrible hotel? Be sure
to recommend it to every guidebook and website
you can find. There is no reason why you should
be the only one to have a crummy vacation.

## SCRATCH GAME

·
·

Here's some entertainment for a crowded commuter journey. Constantly scratch yourself in a way that no one could mistake. Perhaps even take out flea powder in a showy way. Fellow travelers will soon give you a wide berth.

## ME NO SPEEKEE ENGLISH

!

If an unwary foreigner approaches you seeking information in broken English, pretend you don't understand a word they say. Keep up the pretense of utter incomprehension for a good ten minutes. Only when they are completely exhausted tell them what they need to know.

## IT'S UP HIS SLEEVE

Magicians always appreciate it if you wander onto the stage and start poking among their props, giving away where they are hiding their rabbits and handkerchiefs. You don't need to spend years perfecting your craft to become every bit as entertaining as they are.

## NOW WASH YOUR HANDS

If you encounter a public restroom that still uses the roller towel, pull the towel all the way to the end. That way everyone else will have to dry their hands on the germ-infested wet bit at the end.

## HEAVEN FROM PENNIES

Go to one branch of your bank and ask for a thousand dollars in coins. Next haul your coins to another bank and ask for the coins to be turned into one dollar bills. Then go to a third branch and deposit them, watching the teller painstakingly count to a thousand. You can either keep this up indefinitely or you can get a life.

# ONE OF THESE LEGS IS NOT LIKE THE OTHER

Whenever you go to a restaurant, stuff some folded-up pieces of paper under one of the legs of the nearest empty table. When the customers arrive, it is a real treat to watch them attempt to eat their meal at a wobbly table.

# DARLING ROVER

Whenever you see a woman with a baby and a dog, always single out the dog and tell her how cute it is, completely ignoring the baby. The look of growing surprise and dismay on the mother's face is absolutely priceless.

## YOU'VE HAD THEIR CHIPS

Learn to play poker well but always pretend that you are just a beginner. Be sure to fleece anyone who dares to patronize you.

# • PARTIES •

## IT'S MY PARTY AND I'LL CRY IF I WANT TO

## BIG PANTS

Be rude to a woman at a party, but surprise her with it. Compliment her: "Fabulous dress! Just beautiful!" Then get her with the insult: "But have you tried control top panty hose?" That'll teach her to make an effort.

## GUESS WHO

Go up to someone at a party and congratulate them on wearing a costume. Try to guess what it is. "Are you Superman? Little Red Riding Hood? Big Bird?" Ignore their protests that they are wearing regular party clothes. Harass them all night. "I know, you're Frankenstein!"

## PLAIN DRESS REQUIRED

Have a party and tell the invitee you dislike most that it is to be a costume party. When they arrive dressed as a clown or whatever, deny you told them it was a costume party. Tell them that if you had meant to have a costume party surely everyone else would be in costume.

## OOPS, SORRY

Pretend you have a nervous tic and repeatedly spill your wine on the other guests. A nice big splash on your hostess's rug would be fun. If you keep apologizing profusely, your host will feel guilty as well as furious.

## BAD TASTE

Tell the host of the party that the food has a funny taste. Profess worry that other guests might get food poisoning. Harangue the host all night. Every time you catch their eye mime clutching your stomach and looking ill.

## GOOD SEAT

:

At your next birthday party, seat everyone next to people they hate. Watch with joy as the party fails miserably. Happy Birthday to You!

# IN THE CLOSET

**!**

At the office Christmas party flirt outrageously with about half a dozen of the most desperate single people and then tell them to meet you in the supplies closet for a rendezvous. The closet should fill up with a group of same-sex coworkers in a very amorous mood.

# HOW OLD ARE YOU NOW?

•
•

At the next birthday party you go to, ask the birthday girl how old she is in front of everybody. When she hesitates to answer, guess her age loudly, adding fifteen years.

## PLONKER

Bring a cheap bottle of wine, but when you get to
the party switch it with something good that
someone else bought. Then brag loudly about
your superior sommelier skills.

## HEARTBREAKER

Try to seduce someone who is already in a relationship. You can't be truly mean unless you break up at least one couple a month. You get extra points if you split up the same couple more than once.

## HAPPY NEW YEAR?

At the next New Year's Eve party, go around the house and change all the clocks by a few minutes. This will ensure arguments and confusion as to the exact time to toast midnight.

## SWEET SIXTEEN

Invite all your daughter's friends over for her sixteenth birthday. Hire a children's clown to entertain them, and then suggest they play Pin the Tail on the Donkey. Have cake and milk for refreshments. She may eventually forgive you, if she doesn't die of embarrassment first.

# EMPTY PROMISE

At parties, always carry an empty but visible packet of cigarettes. When desperate smokers ask you for a cigarette you can take great pleasure in opening your packet and saying, "Oh, I'm out too." There is nothing so enjoyable as observing the pointless craving of the hardened tobacco addict.

# IDENTITY CRISIS

Have fun at business gatherings by asking for the business card of the first person you talk to, then pretend to be that person to the next person you talk to, exchanging cards again at the end of that conversation. By the end of the night you should have taken on the identity of a dozen or so people and sown utter confusion among the guests.

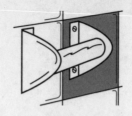

## USE A PAGE FROM THIS BOOK

If the party is at someone's house, the first thing you do is go into each and every one of the bathrooms and hide ALL the toilet paper. This will definitely put a damper on the party. Be sure to replace all the rolls at the end of the evening. The hosts will be extra confused.

## LAVATORY HUMOR

∙
∙

A good way to sabotage a toilet at a party is to unhook the lever from the water release mechanism. To everyone's discomfort, the fact that the toilet will no longer flush should keep embarrassed users trapped in the bathroom for what will seem like an eternity.

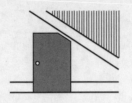

SURPRISE!

Invite all your friends over for a surprise party. When your guests arrive ask them to hide in the closet, saying you will signal them when to yell, "Surprise!" After many hours open the closet door and tell them it is time to go home.

## CALL ME

Plant phone numbers in the coat pockets of your gentlemen guests. The name "Samantha" written in lipstick should cause consternation when found by a prying wife.

WALLFLOWER

!

Bring a friend who knows no one to a party. As
you run into person after person, greet them
excitedly, talk, catch up, but never introduce the
friend. At the end of the evening introduce
your friend to the most attractive person there,
but then hurry them away saying it's time to go.

## SHARE YOUR CULTURE

**:**

Or specifically: At a holiday party, bring a friend who you know does not celebrate that holiday. Spend the night introducing them to people, eagerly volunteering that they are of another faith and don't celebrate like all the rest of us.

# AS PURITAN AS THE DRIVEN SNOW

Have a big party and invite all your friends. But instead of including fun and drinks, try to convert them to your new religion, your new religion being Puritanism.

## NOT OPEN ALL NIGHT

Are you at a party with lots and lots of beer bottles? It is your civic duty as a mean person to hide the bottle opener. Be sure to grab the corkscrew too. What a joy it is to watch partiers search fruitlessly for a way to get at the alcohol.

## WERE WE THERE?

•
•
•

Offer to videotape your friend's wedding. Make
sure you have no footage of the bride or groom,
and offer only fleeting glimpses of their family.
Be sure, though, to include plenty of footage of
the caterers, the band, and people's feet.

## WEAR RUBBER

Invite your friends to an S&M party, and give
them the address of the local church. Imagine
what they'll ask the minister to do.

## CARELESS WHISPER

Have a surprise party for one of your friends. While everyone is hidden, encourage the guest of honor to talk indiscreetly about some of the guests. Once they have disrespected three or four guests, shout "Surprise!"

## BAD COMPANY

Does your spouse want you to accompany them to their important office party? Spice things up by wearing a really inappropriate wig such as "big hair" or long, silky blonde hair, and dressing as a hooker or pimp.

## LOST YOUR MARBLES

⦂

Think people are going to look into your medicine cabinet at your next party? Fill it with marbles, and the first person who snoops will cause a tremendous ruckus. You, of course, will be standing right outside the bathroom door to greet your red-faced guest.

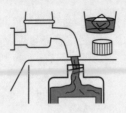

# PROHIBITION

At your next party serve non-alcoholic beer, substitute the vodka with water, and serve grape juice instead of wine. Then watch your guests get drunk anyhow, because they are too stupid to notice the difference.

## BY INVITATION ONLY

Crash some stranger's wedding and pretend to be a long-lost relative who wasn't invited. Tell everyone how hurt you are to have been excluded. If you do this well you may even get an apology from the bride herself.

## LOST AND FOUND

Enjoyed the party you were invited to last night?
Don't forget to phone your hostess. Not to thank
them, but to report that you've lost an earring.
Call every couple of hours asking if they've found
it yet. When you think they've turned their house
upside down, you can call and say you've found it.

## BEFORE AND AFTER

Attending a christening for a child you deem unattractive? Arrive with a full array of cosmetics and beauty treatments, gleefully shouting, "It's time for a baby makeover!"

## THE PREMIERE

Are you having a christening for your child?
Be sure to show the video of the birth to all of
the godparents. They really want to see it,
they're just too shy to ask. On second thought,
show it to everyone!

## LITTLE PERSON

At the next dinner party you have, make sure that one of your chairs is much smaller than the rest, and seat in that chair the most opinionated and obnoxious of all your guests. The guest, being smaller than the rest, will spend the evening looking like a shouting child.

## THE SACRIFICE

!

Have you been made a godparent and want to tease the parents about your potential as a religious guardian? Arrive at the christening with devil horns and a sacrificial goat. Oh, how everyone will laugh!

## GLASSES RAISED

:

Offer to make a toast at the next wedding you go
to. Be sure to use the name of the groom, but
don't use the right name for the bride, calling
her instead by the name of the groom's ex.
Toasting the bride and groom but substituting
the bride's name with the groom's first love
should set the tone for the honeymoon.

## IT'S NO SURPRISE

Is someone throwing a surprise party? Make sure you time your arrival at the exact time as the guest of honor. (This means you'll probably have to hide in the bushes.) As you ring the doorbell just say, "I don't really know the guy having a surprise party, how about you?"

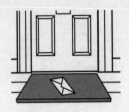

# PARTY PLANNER

Send out beautiful invitations to a black tie party to be held at the swankiest hotel in town. Tell everyone you have hired a great band, the food will be the best, and the champagne will be flowing. Lead your guests to believe it will be the party of the year. Of course, you will cancel on the day, because you never actually did anything.

# THE UNPARTY

•
•

If you're throwing a bachelor party, instead of having a stripper and huge amounts of booze, have an AA counselor and a priest. Your guests will really appreciate the chance to come clean about all their addictions. Certainly no one will resent you for taking away the only fun night they might have all year.

## PARTY OF TWO

•
•

Next time you are invited to a party, turn up a day early. Your host will feel obliged to invite you in anyway, and you will accept, forcing your host to entertain you. Your mission as a mean person is to eat and drink all the food and liquor reserved for the party.

## I'M STUFFED

.
.
.

If you are invited to a dinner party where you
know the hostess will be going to a lot of trouble
making preparations, be sure to have a big meal
before you arrive. That way you won't be able to
eat any of your hostess's lovingly-made food. Just
keep saying, "Oh I couldn't, I had a huge lunch."

# I WAS ONCE GEORGE WASHINGTON

Stay too long at a dinner party. Way too long. If you see your hosts trying to stay awake by slapping themselves silly, stay even longer. Don't leave until you have told your entire life story, including all your past-life experiences.

# BE A WEIGHT WATCHER

Got a fat friend on a diet? Invite her to a dinner party where you will serve luscious food to all your guests, except your dieting friend who will receive lettuce leaves and a carrot. Tell her how proud you are of her that she is finally addressing her weight problem, as you chomp on your lasagna. Mmm, time for dessert...

## DEATHWATCH

If you are going to a costume party, dress as the Grim Reaper. Be sure to spend the entire night reminding people of their eventual death. If someone escapes your attention and is having a good time, you and your scythe should get over there immediately and tell these people that they are going to die. Soon.

## HERE COMES THE BRIDE

If you are throwing a bachelor party, hamper the groom's enjoyment by hiring a stripper who looks like the bride. The groom will spend all night feeling guilty, though the other guests will undoubtedly feel strangely titillated.

# PARTY ON DUDE

Invite everyone who has ever been horrible to you to a party. Get them all in a room together, then sneak out and lock them in. Since they are all nasty, annoying people, you will have the pleasure of knowing that they can now only be nasty and annoying to each other. Leave them to duke it out for as long as is legally possible.

# • THE OFFICE •

## WORKING OVERTIME ON BEING MEAN

# DA VINCI IS IN THE BUILDING

!

Has your colleague been working on an important report for ages? Insert the phrase, "Help me, I'm stuck in an office job and I've got the soul of an artist!" sporadically throughout the document just before it is printed up.

## OBSESSIVE COMPULSIVE DISORDER

Take revenge on the insanely well-organized person by randomly moving their files around. Simply go into their filing cabinet and put every tenth file somewhere else. Watch them agonize over an A file being in the D section as they wonder if they're going insane.

# NO PARKING

Is your boss feeling insecure about their job? Paint out the name in their parking space and then replace it with the name of that ambitious person from Accounts. Then sit back and enjoy as the boss panics for the rest of the day.

# SMOKING KILLS

Is your coworker always on a smoking break? Cheerfully answer their phone for them the next time they are on one, but give out incorrect information, which they will then have to spend hours sorting out. As they become more stressed, they will need more cigarette breaks, giving you ample opportunity to cause more chaos.

## PUBLIC SPEAKING

Randomly insert a picture of a scantily clad woman into your chosen victim's PowerPoint presentation, and then watch as they try to explain it to two hundred people.

## SNAPPY SNAPS

Next time you go on vacation take about sixty pictures of the sunset and bring them to the office. See how long coworkers can continue to fabricate appreciative comments about the same thing, and observe the evermore desperate attempts to hide their boredom.

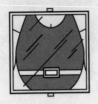

# MIRROR MIRROR ON THE WALL

Replace the mirror in the women's bathroom with a mirror that makes them seem fatter than they are. If someone stares miserably at themselves for more than a minute, you can consider this act of meanness a success.

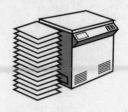

# SORRY I'VE USED UP THE TONER

Keep an eye peeled for when someone needs to use the photocopier urgently. This is the time for you to nip in ahead of them and copy that 300-page document that you've been dreading. Your own boredom will be relieved by your chuckles.

## GREEN DAY

If the office vegetarian is pissing you off with their anti-meat rants, why not inject some liver paté into their pasta salad? Then ask them how it is, and enjoy as they reply: "Mmm... don't know why, but it seems extra delicious today."

## OUT OF ORDER

Block the toilet. Don't report it to anyone. Deny all responsibility if interrogated.

# I KNOW WHAT YOU DID LAST NIGHT

**:**

The day after the office party, go around to various people and congratulate them on some piece of invented outrageous behavior, such as dancing naked except for a tie. When they say they don't remember, chuckle knowingly and say: "Don't worry, everyone else in the office does! Especially the Managing Director."

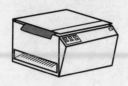

# RELOCATION, RELOCATION, RELOCATION

Print up a document entitled, "Secret: For Management Eyes Only. Proposed Relocation of the Office to Bratislava." Leave it on the photocopier for someone to find.

# GOOD DAY FOR A G'DAY

Tell the receptionist that the boss is thinking of replacing her with an Australian because they have a friendlier accent. Advise her that to avoid being fired she should start answering the phone with an Aussie accent.

## QUITTING TIME

Prepare a lengthy "Things to do by Tomorrow" list. But do not give it to your assistant until you see them getting ready to go home. It is extra satisfying to do this on a day when you know that your assistant has a big date.

# THE POST-IT WITH THE MOST IT

Write an important memo to your assistant on a post-it note. Make the letters small and illegible. Occasionally have a word they can understand, such as "and" or "the," just to give them a small sense of achievement.

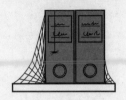

## THE PAPER CHASE

Send your assistant on a wild goose chase. Tell them that you need to find a file that should be on your computer somewhere. Give them just a few key words to start from, such as "client," "payment," and "ten years ago."

# MEETING NOT SO CUTE

Boss been taking you for granted recently? Take a couple of days off, but before you go, schedule a 5 a.m. meeting, and a 2 a.m. overseas conference call at his home that he won't know about until the phone rings.

## YOUR MISSION SHOULD YOU
## CHOOSE TO ACCEPT IT

Give your assistant an "important" assignment.
Tell them it absolutely must be done by the end
of the day. Watch them rush around. When they
arrive panting at 5:29 with the assignment
finished, calmly tell them that you won't need it
until next week after all.

## RUSSIAN ROULETTE

How about inserting a single laxative among the office box of chocolates? Working out who has eaten the explosive candy should relieve a little boredom, and you can make private bets with yourself as to who is the victim.

SMOKIN'

Put a no-smoking sign on the door of the Smoking Room. Then place a "Smoking Room" sign on the boss's office door.

## MAGNIFYING GLASS

Hand your assistant a very long document and tell them to make the amendments you've marked in the text. Except, of course, there aren't any. You can take it back from them after they've wasted a few days looking and developed a haunted expression of despair.

## ICY MEETING

Ask a friend to call up a member of the sales team and arrange a meeting with them, preferably somewhere far away. Then enjoy the thought of your victim sitting miserably in a hotel lounge in Anchorage, Alaska.

## OH, HI CHANTELLE

Miss no opportunity to call your boss's wife by his mistress's name (or something suitably suggestive: Fantasia, Candy, Mrs. Whip, etc...). Make sure that you sound flustered and awkward after you've done it.

## LIVE LONG AND PROSPER

Does someone think they're the coolest person in the office? Subscribe to *Star Trek Fact Files* from Europe in their name and have it sent to them at the office. Watch them try to convince your coworkers that they aren't a nerd. (However, if you know what *Star Trek Fact Files* are, you're pretty nerdy yourself.)

## HELP WANTED

!

Leave the "Career Opportunities" page open on your victim's desk, where his or her boss will see it. Make sure that jobs with major rival companies are circled clearly in red ink.

## OUT TO LUNCH

Is your assistant just about to go to lunch? Tell them you need to speak to them for a moment, and that you'll be right there. Then go out for a merry lunch. When you return your assistant will still be waiting at their desk. Oh, the power!

## OUT TO LUNCH REVENGE

Surreptitiously spray your boss's coat with tacky perfume before he leaves the office. Imagine him going home and having to explain to his wife why he smells like a cheap whore.

## SOCIAL WHIRL

Give the office Casanova a poke in the eye. Glue
the pages for the next four weeks in his calendar
together, and watch how his cool slips as he tries
to arrange yet another date over the phone.

ENIMEN

Simply pop out the "m" and "n" keys on someone's keyboard and transpose them. Then just sit back and watch your coworker go purple with rage as they try to write a memo.

# HAIR TODAY, GONE TOMORROW

Here's a delicious prank for an office coworker, paranoid about losing his hair. Ask a hair salon for any old hair clippings the same color as your victim's, and keep leaving clumps around where he sits. Stand back and watch the paranoia grow.

## RE: A LITTLE HUMOR TO BRIGHTEN YOUR DAY

Do you have a coworker who thinks they are the hilarious office joker? Send an e-mail to everyone from their computer—a horrible and unfunny bad-taste joke. Follow it up with their resignation letter. If you are caught just tell them that with their brilliant sense of humor you were sure they'd find it funny.

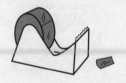

## A STICKY END

Don't you just hate those organized people who like to fold over the end of their Scotch tape roll? Make it your life's work to go around with scissors snipping off the ends, so they have to pick away with their fingernails like the rest of us.

DICTIONARY

Give your office rival a "Word A Day" calendar. Only this will be one you make yourself. Use real words, but give them the wrong definition. For instance: "Officious—pleasant and charming, a good compliment for the boss." Or how about: "Obsequious—honest and dedicated. A good word to describe yourself in an interview situation."

## BLACK ON BLACK

•

Fix a coworker's computer font color so that it types black writing onto a black background. Then remove the font color button from the toolbar. Watch them try everything to fix it. After a few hours, fix it when they step away from their desk. Every so often, do it again.

# NUTRITIONAL SUPPLEMENT

Sabotage the smug office dieter for a month by adding weight-gain formula to their Lo-Cal Soup powder. They will be horrified to find that their diet has resulted in weight gain rather than loss, and they may stop boasting about it for a while.

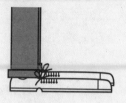

## CLOWNING AROUND

If you are the boss, you are in a uniquely powerful position to be mean. For example, instead of "Dress Down Friday," why not introduce "Clown Dress Friday," in which your staff have to turn up to work dressed in silly costumes. The only problem is that far from finding this humiliating, some people may actually enjoy it.

# YOU'RE FIRED

Today, at noon, fire somebody. Then, at five past noon, tell that staff member that it was a case of mistaken identity, and that the corporate office will send the name of the person who is really to be sacked later today. That will freak out one person for a short time, and freak everybody else out for the rest of the day.

## SAFE TRAVELING

Away on a business trip with coworkers? Plant condoms in your coworker's suitcase. This should hopefully raise suspicions at home.

# FINDERS KEEPERS, LOSERS WEEPERS

Quit your job. On your last day, hide the report you've been working on in the coffee room, put all your files under the filing cabinet, and glue your desk drawers shut. That'll teach those bastards to put any faith in you.

# • FRIENDS AND NEIGHBORS •

HE MAKES NO FRIENDS WHO NEVER MADE A FOE

# A NICE BRIGHT ORANGE

Paint your house a hideous color. Sure it will bother you, but it will bother your annoying neighbors even more. You only have to look at the color as you are walking up to the house. They will have to look at it ALL the time.

## KING TUT

How lovely it is when friends have you over for dinner. It seems churlish not to spoil the mood. Insist, therefore, on washing the cutlery you've been given before you eat with it, tutting loudly, and examining the plates closely for food stains.

ZIG A ZIG AH

Borrow your friend's cell phone and download a really embarrassing ring tone. Imagine their horror when their phone rings on a crowded train playing a medley of Spice Girl songs.

## MONKEY STATUE

Do you have an annoying friend who is getting married? Buy them the most grotesque present you can imagine, like a big statue of a monkey. Bring it to them and have them open it in front of you. The fun part is watching them trying to find something nice to say about it.

# THE FUN IS OVER

Has your friend just been promoted? Bring them down to earth by reminding them of the work, loss of popularity, incredibly long hours, and gray hairs that extra responsibility brings.

## MOTHER THERESA

If you have been promoted you should brag about it at every opportunity. Then, go up to the friend who earns the least and patronizingly offer to lend them money. Tell them you are glad you are in a position to "help."

## PLEASE SIR I WANT SOME MORE

Has your best friend just lost a load of weight and looks terrific? You can either grit your teeth in jealousy or sabotage them. Tempt them daily with baked goods, fine wines, and delicious treats. Force all those calories into them, telling them they look so good they can afford to ease up a bit. Do not stop until they are fat again.

## BROWN DIAMONDS, LUCKY YOU

If you are a woman and your best friend gets engaged, under no circumstances are you to admire the ring. Whip out the magnifying glass you keep for such occasions. Your duty is to find flaws, both in the actual ring and the style of the setting. And while you're at it, criticize the fiancé.

## GO DUTCH

If you are a man and your best friend gets engaged you have no recourse but to say, "Oh that's great. She's fantastic in bed. Really wild. Why, just last week we slipped off to Amsterdam together..."

## BANGING THE HEADBOARD

:

Whenever you have sex, make sure it is good and loud. The neighbors must think your sex life is wild and wonderful. Don't let them suspect that you are dull and dreary. And never let them suspect you are single.

## BABY TALK

Next time you're on the phone with a friend, ask them if they want to speak to your child. Ignore their protests and put little Johnny on the phone. Leave them to listen to your kid's mumblings and whining for as long as you like.

## TALK TO HIM

Want to get back at a friend who made you talk to their kid? Next time they put little Johnny on the phone tell the kid he's adopted. And you're sleeping with his father.

YOU HAVE NO NEW MESSAGES

Never pass an answering machine without deleting every third message. This will add a welcome element of randomness to its owner's otherwise dull and uneventful life.

# THE GRASS IS ALWAYS GREENER

Whenever your next-door neighbor buys something new, always get the same thing only a later
version. If they get a flat screen TV, you get an
HDTV. If they get a BMW, you get a Jag. It will
drive them crazy. You will go into debt, but no
one said that being mean is cheap.

# MENSA

**!**

Play a game with your friends. Ask them to estimate each other's IQs by secretly writing them on pieces of paper. Then, surreptitiously replace most of the pieces of paper with suggestions under 100. Observe the consternation of the dimwits as they argue with each other.

## DON'T SAY ANYTHING

When in conversation with a friend, why not choose a random word to be upset by. When your friend enquires why you have burst into tears at the word "cheese," invent a childhood catastrophe involving some cheese that has scarred you for life. Imagine the fun to be had inventing traumas for all sorts of harmless words.

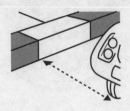

# DON'T EVEN THINK OF PARKING HERE

Do you have a friend who is nervous about parallel parking? Offer to help but then over-exaggerate how close they get to hitting the other cars, and keep making them start over because they got the angle wrong. They should be a nervous wreck by the time you've finished, with their parking confidence ruined forever.

## OPEN HOUSE

⋮

Place a small ad in the local newspaper advertising a room to rent at a bargain rate in your victim's house. Be sure to include their work and home phone numbers, plus e-mail address, so that they get bombarded for days.

## AIR YOUR DIRTY LAUNDRY

•
•
•

Do you live in a snooty neighborhood? There is
nothing rich people hate more than a laundry
line, so be sure to hang yours high and proud
and to adorn it with the most garish and
embarrassing items of underwear you can find.

## STICK IT TO THE KIDS

Teach those kids next door a lesson. Glue some coins to the sidewalk outside your house, and watch them struggle and whine when they think they've got lucky and try to pick them up.

## PACK ANIMAL

Are you going on a long hike with someone?
Make sure you pack some of your heaviest things
in your friend's backpack. No reason to risk
injuring your own spine.

# FETCH LITTLE JOHNNY FETCH

Is your friend bragging about their new baby?
When they tell you all the tricks little Johnny can
do, act excited and tell them that Johnny has
almost caught up with your new puppy, Patches.

# WHERE'S MY KENNY ROGERS?

Never visit a house without sneaking CDs into different boxes. Imagine the ensuing fight when the obsessive husband yells at his wife to put the CDs back properly and she swears on a stack of Bibles that she did.

## MEMORIES

Are you envious that your best friend is getting married? Bring as your date the one person who broke their heart and they haven't quite gotten over. Wouldn't it be a hoot if your friend actually said the wrong name at the altar?

## DON'T ASK DON'T TELL

Sick of your friends asking when you are going to have kids? Next time they ask, just say, "Well, after looking at yours I'm too revolted to even think about it." Problem solved.

## LATE TO BED, EARLY TO RISE

•
•
•

Next time you go to a friend's house, slip into the bedroom and change the setting of their alarm clock, so that it goes off at 4:30 a.m., instead of their usual lazy 7:30. Then you can have great delight in imagining them stumbling out of bed, bleary-eyed and confused, as they set off to work in the dark.

## SUGAR RUSH

**⋮**

When you visit friends who have kids, be sure to bring lots of sugary treats for the lovely children. Play with them until they are wildly overexcited. At this exact point, make your excuses and depart, leaving the parents to cope with the newly unleashed mania. You might want to go back an hour later to stoke it all up again.

## RING A DING

·
·

At the movies, when you are reminded to turn off your cell phone, reach into your companion's bag and turn their cell phone back on. At a suitably dramatic moment, secretly call their number from your own phone. Not only is it mean to your friend, it's also mean to the audience.

## CAN'T GET IT UP

Your neighbor has just bought an expensive new bread-making machine and invites you over to help christen it. Sneak over early and replace their yeast supply with talcum powder. Then enjoy their deflation and humiliation as the bread refuses to rise. Being gracious, you can say that you'd love to taste it anyway...

# THE DEVIL MADE ME DO IT

New neighbors just moved in? Invite them over for a welcome drink. Before they arrive, light hundreds of candles and draw a giant chalk pentagram on the floor. When the doorbell rings greet them in robes and hand them goblets of a suspicious red liquid. (Be wary if they don't run away immediately. They may actually be Satanists.)

# EVERY PICTURE TELLS A STORY

•
•
•

Take some pictures of your friend and pick out the very worst one, which makes them look horrible, and give it to them saying, "I think this photo makes you look so good." When they protest, say, "No, it really is an excellent likeness. I don't see how you could expect better."

## MUSEUM OF MODERN ART

•
•
•

When visiting the house of a person who is ostentatiously showing off their prized abstract artwork to a crowd of visitors, casually point out that you are an expert on that artist's work and that this painting has been hung upside down. Then suggest that the owner's face is now a shade of red that reminds you of Monet's poppies.

# HERE'S YOUR HAT, WHAT'S YOUR HURRY?

Do you have a houseguest who is staying too long?
How about putting something under the mattress
that will make it uncomfortable. A hammer is
good, or a basketball, or better yet, try their
suitcase, with their stuff already packed in it.

## THE NAKED LUNCH

Houseguest still outstaying their welcome? Try walking around naked and telling the guest that the new rules are that everybody in the house has to be naked all the time. But make sure your guest leaves. The only thing worse than a houseguest who stays too long, is a houseguest who stays too long who is naked.

# EVERYONE'S A CRITIC

Has your obnoxious friend just published their novel? Go to Amazon.com and write a bad review of their book. Give it no stars. This is one that will give immediate gratification because authors check their Amazon reviews hourly.

## CHERRY ON THE CAKE

Bake a delicious-looking cake, lusciously frosted and beautifully decorated, and invite people over to share it. Of course, you neglect to put sugar in, so the cake will have no flavor whatsoever. Not only do you get to hear guests politely insist how good it tastes, but you get to watch their little faces crumple in disappointment.

## RISE AND SHINE

Has your neighbor been kind enough to allow you to borrow something? Return the item at five in the morning. Your neighbor will really appreciate the early start.

## DEAR DIARY

Always take the opportunity to insert fake appointments in people's diaries. If you copy their handwriting style effectively, you will not only have them scurrying around all over the place, but also doubting their sanity.

## SHOW CONCERN

The simplest, easiest, no-effort way to be utterly mean to a woman requires saying just three little words: You Look Tired.

# RAINDROPS KEEP FALLING ON MY HEAD

Always keep umbrellas in the house to hand out to friends in need. Of course, you have previously made minuscule holes in these umbrellas to let the water in. There is nothing so good as being mean while appearing generous.

## THE OTHER SIDE OF ATKINS

Lose lots of weight and when everyone asks you your secret, invent a bogus diet that includes bread, butter, and loads of sugar. Your friends will get fatter as you stay slim.

## WAIT UNTIL DARK

Save all your dead lightbulbs and the packaging they come in. Then you can plant them in other people's houses, ensuring that everyone will always have a supply of useless lightbulbs to confuse them. (This works for batteries, too.)

## MINIMUM WAGE

Become friendly with all the neighborhood kids.
They are a great source of free labor.

## WET DREAM

Someone unfashionable enough to still have a waterbed deserves your attention. And the attention of your scissors.

# HAVE A TIC TAC

⋮

Always have breath fresheners handy, and, with a concerned face, offer them to people. This should have everyone you know trying to smell their own breath in a paranoid manner.

# A SCREAMING GOOD TIME

:

Train your kid to have a giant tantrum on your
say-so. Then whenever you see anyone having a
good time, let your kid loose.

## MOMMY AND DADDY AREN'T HOME

**⋮**

Always use your child's voice as the outgoing message on your voicemail. Your friends and acquaintances are always happy to hear the constant reminders of your fertility.

## SPECIAL NEEDS

:

If your friend has the audacity to have their child as the outgoing message on their answering machine, you should have the audacity to leave a message hinting that little Susie may not have met all her developmental goals.

## SCHOOL SPIRIT

If you are going to a school reunion it is IMPERATIVE that you make everyone there feel bad about their lives. Brag about your houses and cool career which has made you rich. Be sure to show up in a BMW, wearing expensive clothes and dripping gold jewelry, even if you have to rob a bank to do so.

# THERE IS A FREE LUNCH

When next dining out with a friend, pretend you are going to the bathroom and simply leave. As you depart, stop at the cash register and tell the cashier that your friend will pay. Give your friend a cheery wave, and they'll wave back, setting the cashier's mind at rest.

## ORCHESTRAL MANEUVERS

Take up a musical instrument, preferably the tuba. Your neighbors will really appreciate how loud noises and vibrations coming through the walls enhance their cultural life. Of course they may return the favor and take up the saxophone.

# YOU SHOULD HAVE GONE 50/50

If your friend is on *Who Wants To Be a Millionaire?* and asks you to be their "phone a friend" be sure to supply them with the wrong answer. Hey, who wants a friend who is richer than they are?

## THE OMEN

If one of your friends has a child that has been behaving badly, give your friend a big hug and offer these words of comfort: "Don't worry. Some people are just bad seeds. They're born that way. Maybe your next child will be better."

# THE BOOK CLUB

Are you a member of a book club? When it is your turn to suggest something, recommend *Ulysses* by James Joyce, or *Remembrance of Times Past* by Proust. Or *War and Peace*. The point is, they will have to spend weeks trying to read something incredibly long and dull, while you will be phoning the day before the meeting to say you can't make it.

## MY LIFE IS PERFECT

Call your best friend right now and tell them that you just sold your first novel for several million dollars, you have met the love of your life, and you are moving together into the perfect house in the perfect neighborhood. Tell them you have finally found true happiness. Really, nothing could be meaner than this.

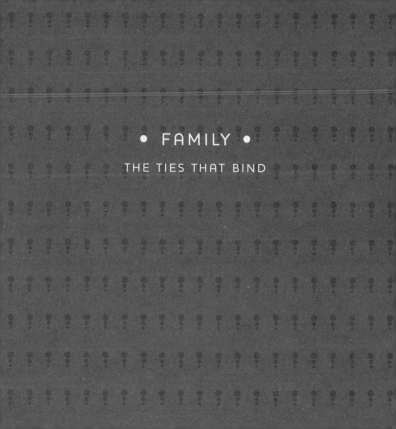

• FAMILY •

THE TIES THAT BIND

GOOD LUCK

The first time you take your new love to another one of your crazy family gatherings don't introduce them to anybody. Just bring them and leave them to fend for themselves. If they still love you after a stunt like that, they are a keeper.

# I'VE GOT A SISTER?

Send an e-mail to everyone in your family telling
them how much you love them, but leave out one
person, preferably the sibling with the lowest
self-esteem. When they ask why you didn't
include them, say, "Oh, I forgot you existed."

## PLAIN BROWN WRAPPER

Stumped for something to buy your father for his birthday? Why not get him a subscription to *Penthouse*? Anonymously of course. Imagine the joy it will bring to your parents' household as they have their nightly "Why would you want to look at this garbage?" argument.

# ROSEBUD IS HIS SLED

Rent a movie for the whole family to see, such as *The Sixth Sense*, and as you slide it into the DVD player give away the ending. Say casually, by way of explanation, "By the way, Bruce Willis is dead. He's a ghost. Enjoy the movie."

# I CAN SEE CLEARLY NOW

Did you know that people have different eyesight in each eye? If you don't believe this, why not switch your dad's contact lenses and watch his confusion. Be sure to switch the lenses back at the end of the day after he's taken them out to avoid being found out.

# WHEN ARE YOU GOING TO MAKE ME A GRANDMOTHER?

Has your mother been nagging about when you're going to give her grandchildren? Go to the roughest area in town, waving money, and hire the craziest kids from the wrong side of the tracks to be your "newly adopted children." Once they have spent a fun evening trashing your mother's house she will never nag you again.

## SHOTGUN WEDDING

Is your older sister single? Nothing will stick in her craw more than you getting married first. So get your act together, get out there right now, get engaged, and get married immediately. Boy, will she be a mess on your wedding day.

# NICE DAY FOR A WHITE WEDDING

Irked that your younger sister is getting married first? Wear a wedding dress to her wedding. Of course it is against etiquette and everyone will think you are crazy. But the confusion caused among guests, and the anger inflicted on your sister, will make this a wedding no one will ever forget.

## TOY STORY

Always bring a selection of sex toys with you when you visit members of your family. Planting them where fellow family members will find them ensures red faces all around. Be sure to always point the blame at your sister.

# HAPPY MOTHER'S DAY

Can't think of what to get your mother for
Mother's Day? How about a big box of guilt?
Instead of the usual sweater, point out that she
once missed a school play because she was in the
hospital. Don't forget to remind her that she
missed one of your football games, too.

## JERRY LEWIS IS BRILLIANT, TOO

!

Entertaining distant relatives visiting from overseas is always tiresome. Entertain yourself, therefore, by taking them to see the worst, most tedious show in town, having first described it to your guests as a work of genius. Extra points for you if they pretend to enjoy it, too.

# TWINS

Next time you are having an argument with your sister, stop her cold by telling her she looks and acts exactly like your mother. If they were standing next to each other you wouldn't be able to tell them apart.

# HE BOUGHT ME A CONDO, TOO

Next time you meet up with a sibling rent a really great car, like a Porsche, for the occasion. When they show admiration casually mention, "Dad bought this for me, for being such a great kid." You can always look back with pleasure at the jealous expression on their face, even after they've discovered the truth.

# IT'S THE THOUGHT THAT COUNTS

**!**

Imply to your sister that this year you are buying her something wonderful and expensive for Christmas. Keep dropping hints: "Ooh you're going to love it..." This should encourage her to spend a fortune on your present. She might give you a big screen TV. You, of course, give her slippers.

## HOMEMADE GIFTS ARE THE BEST

Parents, are you sick of your children giving you crummy presents like a pencil holder made of a dishwashing liquid bottle, or a picture of themselves put in a cheap frame stuck with macaroni? On their next birthday give them a picture of you, or an ashtray you made in your pottery class. Watch their bottom lips quiver.

# MOMMIE DEAREST

Write a book about your dysfunctional family. Go on all the talk shows to discuss your horrible childhood so that you become an inspiration to other sufferers. If your nice parents who actually brought you up well cause a fuss, buy them a new house to shut them up.

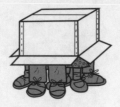

## POINTLESS REVENGE

Have children but never allow your parents to see them. This will break their hearts, and will give them time to meditate on why they didn't buy you a car for your sixteenth birthday.

## CUT IT OUT

Staying at your parents' house? Take one of their sheets and fold it small, then cut into it, as if you're making a snowflake. When your mom sees it she may be angry at first, but eventually she will appreciate your art. (Just like she did when you were five years old.)

## PUNKED

Stick some green vegetable dye in your parent's shampoo. Hey, they criticized punk first time around, and now they can see what they missed.

## DO YOU WANT FRIES WITH THAT?

Take the money you've saved up for your child's education and buy them a car instead. They will appreciate that more than college, and you'll have lots of money left over for yourself. The full implications of this mean act will not be realized by your child until they are well into adulthood going from one crappy job to the next.

# BILLY ELLIOT, NOT

Do you want your son to have a miserable time?
Send him to school in pink lycra, just once. This
single, simple one act of meanness will live with
him for the rest of his life.

# BOOK OF THE DEAD

Is one of your parents having an operation? Set up the recovery room to look as if it is a dark tunnel with a bright light at the end. Then you can say in a soothing voice, "Go toward the light, go toward the light."

# THE RHYTHM METHOD

Give your nephew a drum kit for his birthday. Be sure not to stint on the cymbals. Just think how much his parents will be thrilled by the constant practice of their very own budding Keith Moon.

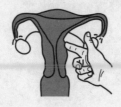

## MY FALLOPIAN TUBES

**:**

If you are a woman, freak your father out by talking about your gynecological ailments. Be detailed. However, don't be freaked out if he finally feels comfortable discussing his latest prostate examination with you.

## NO BIG BIRD

⋮

Take away your kids' television rights. Not
because it is good for them, but because you can.

# HOLD ON TO YOUR HEART

If your child has just lost their first tooth and is excitedly awaiting their initial visit from the tooth fairy, be sure to warn them not to let the tooth fairy steal any of their other vital organs.

## ARE YOU RELATED TO?

:

If you are the eldest sibling, there is a way to be mean to your younger siblings, but it requires a major initial investment of work. When you are young, do everything you can to be the best student in the school. Your siblings then spend their first eighteen years apologizing for not being as bright and well behaved as you.

## • HOLIDAYS •

### UNLEASH YOUR INNER GRINCH

## ALL THE TRIMMINGS

Invite everyone over for Christmas. Act surprised when they tell you they were expecting food. Tell them you thought the pleasure of your company would be more than enough for them.

# THERE'S NO TOOTH FAIRY EITHER

Obviously you must tell all children under the age of eight there is no Santa Claus. It is your civic duty. They will thank you one day. When the parents angrily confront you, feign ignorance of what you have done; tell them little Johnny must be making up stories again.

## DISAPPOINTMENT IN A BOX

For Christmas, buy something cheap and small for someone you don't like. Beautifully wrap it in the biggest box you can find, and watch your victim's face fall as they open it.

# THE PRESENT TENSE

Ask a close friend for a list of presents that they want for Christmas. Don't buy them anything off that list. Instead, buy them a diet book. And maybe a guide to plastic surgery.

# TRICK OR TREAT

On Halloween, ask an unpleasant woman if she is dressed as a witch. Profess shock when she tells you she isn't wearing a costume. Insist she must be wearing a witch mask, or ask if you can try on her false nose and wart.

## HAPPY NEW YEAR

:

Planning to break up with your partner? Do it on New Year's Eve. There is nothing as cleansing as starting out the New Year unencumbered by the numbskull you somehow found yourself involved with. And the added bonus is your ex will forever have the phrase "stroke of midnight" accompanied by a shudder.

## STAY INSIDE THE LINES

How irritating it is to have to buy a gift for a child you don't really know or care about. Make it enjoyable for yourself by buying something completely wrong for the child's age or gender: an infant's coloring book for a sixteen-year-old boy; a bong for a five-year-old.

## HARDBOILED

At this year's Easter egg hunt, push all the children out of the way and find the Easter eggs yourself. Children can be so slow sometimes. And they are easy to outmaneuver.

# A TOAST TO THE NEW YEAR

This New Year's Eve remain stone cold sober and spend the evening recording all the stupid things that your drunk friends say. Spend the next year plaguing them by playing back the old year's examples of their drunken ramblings.

## HEALTHY SNACKS

Give the trick-or-treaters a real treat this Halloween. Instead of giving them unhealthy candy give them something special. They will really appreciate fresh fruit or raisins. Perhaps even granola. Or Brussels sprouts. Broccoli is always healthy. Mmmm... yummy.

## SCARED YOU DIDN'T I?

Join in with the spirit of Halloween by dressing up yourself. What fun it will be when a group of small children dressed as ghosts and goblins see the big door open, only to be confronted by Freddie Kruger laughing like a maniac.

## FA LA LA

All partygoers love the sound of someone singing Christmas carols. Therefore, learn a selection of songs, and tell everybody that you've always wanted to sing them. Sing them relentlessly but constantly out of key, finish with a beaming smile, and wait expectantly for compliments.

# SANTA CLAUS IS COMING TO TOWN

Go up to a Santa (at a store or collecting money on the street) and present him with your Christmas list. Convince this person that you absolutely believe in him.

## SECRET ADMIRER

If you are in a committed relationship this Valentine's Day, send yourself a lovely, unsigned card. Follow this up with a stunning bouquet of flowers. Make sure that you act suspiciously and laugh rather too loudly when your partner asks if you are having an affair.

## LIT UP

There is nothing more annoying than a neighbor overindulging with Christmas lights. Their attempt to bring joy to the neighborhood by covering their house with thousands of lights and "Santa Rules" adornments cries out for intervention. Creep out in the night and change the display to read "Satan Rules."

## 'TIS THE SEASON

There is nothing more satisfying than being an overenthusiastic neighbor and hanging garish Christmas lights. Hey, why not overdecorate your house for every occasion? Hanukkah, Kwanza, Ramadan—they all deserve your special tacky, nouveau-riche touch.

# KICK HER WHILE SHE'S DOWN

Is your friend depressed because they have been dumped? Be sure to send them a Valentine's card signed from the person who dumped them. Imagine their horror when they hopefully call their ex only to find it was a hoax.

## THE OLD SWITCHAROO

While visiting friends with kids before Christmas sneak away and swap the gift tags on the kids' gifts. Make sure you are there on Christmas morning to observe the tears and tantrums as little Johnny gets a doll and little Susie opens a remote-controlled tank. With luck there will be juicy recriminations between the parents, too.

# ST. VALENTINE'S DAY MASSACRE

:

Tell your Valentine that you are taking them somewhere really special for Valentine's Day, get them really excited, and then take them to Pizza Hut. Tell them that they always seem so happy when they eat pizza, and you are hurt they are so disappointed. Accuse them of preferring an expensive restaurant to you.

## NOT A HAPPY BUNNY

Get up early on Easter morning, eat all the candy left for the children, and leave in their place a pamphlet on the dangers of juvenile obesity.

## SUPERSIZE IT

Give a female friend a clothing present in extra large. When she looks troubled by the size tell her not to worry and that if the garment is not big enough, it also comes in extra extra large.

## BAD CALL

Phone your ex this Valentine's Day and tell them that even if you had the chance to do it over again, you'd still break up with them.

# A PUZZLING PRANK

People love receiving jigsaw puzzles as Christmas gifts. They especially love puzzles from which one key piece has been removed and thrown away by the giver. The frantic searching of their house for the missing piece also gives them great joy, as does the sight of the incomplete picture staring up at them from the table.

## PICTURE PERFECT

This Christmas, give your loved ones a lovely family portrait—the portrait being painted according to your specifications, which means you are clear and attractive and the rest of your family are blurry images revolving around you.

## HARSH REMINDER PART 1

Want to ruin your wife's Christmas? It's easy—
just buy her a Thighmaster.

## HARSH REMINDER PART 2

Want to ruin your husband's Christmas? Simply buy him some Rogaine.

## DADA HALLOWEEN

On Halloween, when the doorbell rings, open it and say, "Trick or Treat." The trick or treaters will be confused and answer back, "Trick or Treat," at which point you say, "Trick or Treat" again. They'll probably say it again. Then you say, "Trick or Treat" again. Don't say anything but "Trick or Treat." You can keep this up all night.

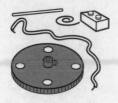

## BATTERIES INCLUDED

Be sure to buy other people's children Christmas presents that look amazing on the box, but will have to be assembled by someone. Make sure it is so complicated the father will have to spend all day putting that damn toy together.

## CHEAP CHEAP

!

Tell everyone you'll be out of town for Christmas. Then do all your shopping when everything is on sale after the holidays. Give out the gifts the following weekend.

# CHARITY BEGINS NOT AT YOUR HOME

Invite some homeless people over for Christmas
dinner. But give them your neighbor's address.

## 'TIS NOT THE SEASON

If you decorate the outside of your house with Christmas lights, why not put them up early this year, say in August. And keep them up really late, say until next June. Remember, the annoyance caused by ostentatious lights is for life, not just for the twelve days of Christmas.

## A SELFLESS ACT

Tell your children that there will be no Christmas presents this year, because you've donated all the money you would have spent on them to poor children.

## CHRISTMAS PRESENT

**:**

Spoil your children's lives forever by only getting pregnant in late March. Everyone knows that people born in December always have their Christmas presents and birthday presents combined, and no one goes out of their way to make them feel special. Extra points if they're born on Christmas Day

# • DATING •

DINNER, A MOVIE, AND MISERY

## BUSY ON FRIDAY?

Ask someone arrogant and conceited on a date. Have them meet you at a restaurant. When they show up, feign confusion. Say "Oh, I didn't realize I was speaking to you. You have the same last name as the person I really wanted to go out with." That'll take them down a peg or two.

## GLEN OR GLENDA?

The next time you're on a dull, uninteresting date, announce that you are a transsexual. Tell your date that you had been wrestling with mixed feelings about your gender for a long time, but that an evening spent in their company has convinced you that you made a mistake.

## SHIVER ME TIMBERS

On your next date dress in an inappropriate costume, such as a pirate or ballerina. Never mention it. When your date asks, look confused and pretend you don't understand. Watch with amusement as they try to invent a plausible excuse to get the hell away from you.

# WE ARE HOT

If you're married, go on a double date with another married couple. You and your spouse should engage in rampant public displays of affection. Brag about how often you do it. You should even go off for a while and come back claiming you had a "quickie." Your friends will feel both embarrassment and envy.

# THE KINSEY REPORT

•
•

Spend an entire date listing all the people you have ever slept with. Don't go off your subject, no matter what. Be specific. Be graphic. Provide intimate details. Bring photos. Say they were all fantastic. Ask your date if they can measure up.

## GET AWAY

If you've been dating someone for a while, spend the evening discussing a romantic vacation for two. Bring brochures and ask their advice on everything. Make decisions together. At the end of the evening thank them for their advice and say that you are going away with someone else.

# EINSTEIN DIDN'T CHOOSE IT

Let your date choose the movie. Roll your eyes when they tell you the title. Sigh and look at your watch throughout. At the end tell them how much you admire their simple tastes. Pat them on the head if you like.

## ARE YOU TALKING TO ME?

Spend all night doing your award-winning impersonation of Robert de Niro, and not from his earlier cool movies. Instead be the fire chief from *Backdraft* and bore your date with fire safety tips. You can also demonstrate how to use a fire extinguisher on your date's car.

## DOUBLE DATE?

Flirt incessantly with the person at the next table
(only if they are on a date, too). Go off and have
sex with them if possible. With luck you can be
mean to two people in one evening.

## WHO ARE YOU?

**!**

Call your date by the wrong name all night. Never waver. When they correct you, contradict them. You can really have some fun by telling a bad story about someone with your date's real name.

## ALL EYES ON THE DATE

At some point during the date stand up and shout indignantly, "How dare you. I am not that kind of person." Make sure everyone hears you. Leave immediately, and let your date face the stares and consequences.

## CLOSE RELATIONS

Tell your date that they look exactly like Roseanne. Ask if they are related. Regardless of how much they protest, keep at it all evening. This act of meanness can be particularly effective if your date is a man.

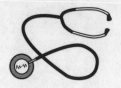

## CALL AN AMBULANCE

If your date is particularly unattractive, fake a heart attack. They can then spend hours waiting for you in the emergency room, while you're flirting with all the cute doctors and nurses.

## CANAL NUMBER FIVE

Find the most disgusting perfume you can find, apply liberally and spend a date claiming how wonderful you smell. As a finale, douse yourself with more of the perfume so you smell truly skunky, and tell your date to take you home right now and make love to you.

## SOULS OF CARROTS

•
•

If your date tells you they are a vegetarian, order a big, juicy steak. Keep offering them bites. Ask them if they eat vegetables, and point out that plants are living beings, too.

## THE VEAL DEAL

If your date orders steak, tell them you are a
vegetarian. Spend the evening regaling them
with horror stories about the meat industry. Cry
when you talk about the poor little cows.

IS THAT YOU?

Develop an olfactory fixation, and spend the evening smelling everything that crosses your path. Keep sniffing in your date's direction, wrinkling your nose and looking displeased.

## TOOTHPICKED

Order a big salad and purposefully get food stuck in your teeth. As your date notices, watch the horror on their face. Pretend you don't understand when they subtly try to let you know. When they finally convince you, spend at least an hour excavating savagely with a toothpick.

# WHAT'S YOUR STAR SIGN?

**!**

Ask your date what star sign they are. When they tell you, shake your head and groan. Spend all evening talking about astrology. Do their chart and make up mean stuff: they will always live with their parents, they will fail at everything, and they are destined to be a serial killer.

# FIGHT CLUB

If you're a woman, when you're next out on a dinner date, pick a fight with the man at the next table. Insult him loudly. Tell him that your date will teach him a thing or two about manners. As soon as the fight starts, get the hell out of there.

## PICK UP THE PHONE

**:**

Keep your cell phone switched on during a date and always answer it: "Hi! Oh, just that date I mentioned... No chance. Call me later; I'll definitely be home early. Bye."

# STRAITJACKET

On a date, keep laughing to yourself, then fall into silent contemplation, where you gaze into the distance with a faraway look in your eyes. When the date asks if anything is wrong, snap out of it, and say, "I think I forgot to take my medication."

## ROLLIN' WITH MY HOMIES

Have your date pick you up at home where a group of cozy friends are hanging out, laughing and talking boisterously. As your date enters, have your friends become silent and stare. Shout to them as you're leaving: "Hope you guys have fun without me, I'm so jealous."

# WAITER, THERE'S A FLY IN MY SOUP

:

On a date, keep finding fault with the restaurant. Change tables three times. Pull things out of your food and say, "Is this a hair?" when it is clearly parsley, or say, "Is this a finger," when it is obviously a parsnip. Show it to the waiter, become sulky and angry, and refuse any offering the date might make to please you.

## A SURE BET

A fun way to get out of a date is to say, "I bet you I can get anyone here to go home with me." Be nice to your date, as you walk out with the bartender, and don't collect on your bet.

## BAD BREATH

Is your new date more looking forward to kissing you than you are to kissing them? Increase their pleasure by ordering tuna, with extra garlic, onions, and curry.

## NEW PLACES

If you are a man who has run out of women to be a "mean date" to, the best place to meet new women is a low self-esteem workshop.

# LET'S BE FRIENDS

·
·

Ask someone out on a date, but when they show up, dressed to the nines and with a look of eager anticipation on their face, explain you are in love with their best friend and you asked them to dinner to get their advice on the matter.

# YOU DON'T LOOK SO GOOD NAKED

:

Is your date particularly obnoxious? Lure them home with a wink and a promise, and ask them to get undressed. Then look them over and say, "Hmm, I don't think so."

## NO SMOKING DAY

If your date is a smoker, tell them you have asthma and close proximity to smoke will hurt you. It is fun to watch them twitch and try to get through their nicotine fits. You, of course, may head off to the bathroom to grab a smoke.

## YOU LOOK GOOD BLURRY

On the next date you go on, wear glasses. In the middle of the date, apropos of nothing, take them off and say, "You look so much better now."

## RECOVERING SEXAHOLIC

Tell your date that you used to be a sex addict, a
wild lover, a shockingly dirty slut. If this were a
year ago, right now you'd be doing unspeakable
things to them under the table. Thankfully, you
are so much better now, you're cured and they
can rest easy, your days of being bad are over.

## PRAY FOR A DATE

Are you a love rat but have earned a reputation in your neighbourhood/local bar/club? Go to church. Lots of women go there to meet nice guys; they'll never suspect a thing.

# FIGARO, FIGARO, FIGARO

Take your date to the opera, something really dull like *The Ring Cycle*. Pretend that you find it really interesting and gratifying and beautiful, which will ensure that your date will feel like a peasant.

## MITTELSCHMERZ

One for the women: In the middle of a date, lean over, blow seductively in your date's ear, and whisper, "I'm ovulating right now." Watch him gallop into the distance.

## I'LL HAVE CAVIAR

Women, don't think of it as a date. Think of it as
a chance to show your desperate needy side and
get a free meal at the same time.

# THE ID, THE EGO, AND THE SUPER EGO

:

Bring a psychology book with you, something like *The Complete Works of Freud*. Every time your date says something, open the book, flick through pages, and furrow your brow. Then look at your date and say, "I see. Very interesting."

## BAT OUT OF HELL

**:**

Instead of taking your date for the traditional dinner followed by a movie, take them to a Meatloaf lookalike contest, in which you have already entered them as a contestant. Women will be especially insulted by this.

# TOO HOT FOR YOU

:

Take your date for an Indian meal, but go armed with a jar of curry powder. When your date goes to reapply her lipstick, you powder her curry. When she complains how spicy it is, look nonchalant, and patronizingly tell her that your palate is just more sophisticated than hers.

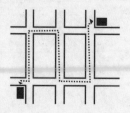

## NARROW ESCAPE

Have your date meet you at a restaurant that has more than one location, tell them to go to the one on Main Street, but of course you'll be at the other one, enjoying a meal unencumbered by the bozo you almost had a date with.

## MEAN FOR LIFE

Be obnoxious all night and let your date know what you are really like. Then propose to them and if they are stupid enough to marry you, go immediately to the "Partners" chapter and proceed to make your spouse's life a misery.

# • PARTNERS •

## 'TIL DEATH DO US PART

WANTED

!

Leave a magazine open at the page where the personal ads are. Circle a few. Make notes in the margins. If queried simply say you wanted to see if you could have done better.

## TAX CHEAT

Report your spouse for tax evasion. Even if they
haven't done anything wrong, you will have weeks
of fun watching them sweat.

## IS THAT YOU, MOM?

**⁝**

Go into your spouse's cell phone and change all their speed dials. Set up all new numbers for them. You get to be mean and make their life interesting all at the same time.

## TOO TOASTY

Put crumbs on your spouse's side of the bed.
When they complain, tell them that they
obviously have a sleep-eating problem.

# NOTICE ANYTHING DIFFERENT?

Drive your spouse insane by continually moving the furniture around. When they complain, insist that no changes have occurred. If necessary, alter a photo of the room on your computer before replacing it in its frame on the mantelpiece to prove that the room has always looked like that.

# SOMEONE HAS PUT ON WEIGHT

Alter your partner's clothes to make them smaller. Your spouse will be convinced they've put on weight. For added meanness, let out your own clothes so they look too loose on you.

## SURPRISE!

Drop subtle clues that you are planning a surprise birthday party for your spouse. Then enjoy their increasing bewilderment when nothing happens on the day.

## DIRTY PHONE CALL

Start having very intense, whispered telephone conversations that you stop when your partner enters the room. Look guilty and evasive. The fact that your were talking to your mother is information that your partner does not need.

# FOGHORN

Complain to your partner about their snoring, when in fact they don't. Tell them you are going to record them to prove it. Play them a wildlife recording of a rutting warthog, then enjoy the discomfort they get from the gadgets they shove up their nose in an effort to please you.

# UNCLEAN! UNCLEAN!

Become a religious freak. Insist that in your new
religion sex is unclean and disgusting.

## JOKUS INTERRUPTUS

Next time your spouse tells a joke, let them struggle through the long setup, and then jump in at the end with the punchline. This works even better if you tell a punchline to a different joke and blame it on your spouse.

## WHO SHOT J.R.?

As a mean partner, it is your sworn duty to miss
the last five minutes of anything your partner
asks you to record for them.

## YOU CAN LOOK BUT YOU BETTER NOT TOUCH

If you're a woman buy some beautiful lingerie and parade it before your spouse. When he gets excited and makes a pass at you, tell him that it will crease your new items and your new underwear is too important to use for mere sex. (You can try this if you're a man, but it may not be so effective.)

# FROM THIS DAY FORWARD

On your wedding night order a huge meal from room service and gobble it down. Continue to eat like a pig on your honeymoon. When your new spouse asks about this, tell them that you had been starving yourself your whole single life, but no longer have to worry about your appearance.

# A MINIATURE VOLCANO

So much meanness can be done with condiments. How about sneaking some crushed Alka-Seltzer into the sugar. Then, when your spouse puts some sugar into their morning coffee you can laugh manically as it bubbles over.

## TOFU AND LENTILS

Announce to your partner that you have both been leading unhealthy lifestyles. Throw out all the alcohol, cakes, and candy. Your partner's face will be priceless when they realize their favorite Jim Beam and Belgian chocolates are gone for good. (You will, of course, hide them away and consume them on your own.)

# THE REMOVAL MAN

:

If your wife is constantly complaining about you leaving the toilet seat up, confuse her by removing it altogether. After that she will be grateful for anything.

OH DEBBIE! OH DEBBIE!

Have sex with your spouse but at a moment of most
intense passion shout out the name of your ex.

## THE WEIGHT IS OVER

Fix the scales one day, so they will show that your spouse has suddenly gained seven pounds. Then a few days later fix them so they show your spouse to be seven pounds lighter. This should set off your loved one on a cycle of bingeing and purging that will be very entertaining.

## THE PUBLIC LITANY

Do you have a list of complaints against your spouse? Save it for when you are next at a family dinner. Your spouse will be humiliated, but your family will enjoy hearing of your spouse's shortcomings, and sometimes it is good to spread the meanness.

## REMOTE CONTROL

Constantly fighting with your partner over what television shows to watch? Go out for a night on the town by yourself and take the television remote with you. Your partner will go insane.

## HIRSUTE

Hair removal is crucial for a healthy relationship. Therefore, you must stop removing yours. If you're a woman, stop shaving your legs and under your arms. If you're a man grow an unkempt beard. Don't stop until you're mistaken for Robinson Crusoe.

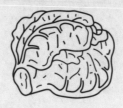

# THE REVENGE DIET

If your husband complains that you have put on weight, go on the "Cabbage Soup" diet. The ensuing flatulence may kill him, and that should teach him not to comment that "you have too much junk in the trunk."

## SUPERBOWL SEX

Withhold sex from your husband for a long period of time, then give him a "once-only" offer of sex during the big game that he's been waiting all week to watch.

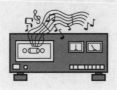

## MIX TAPE

Does your partner have a compilation tape made for them by an ex, which they treasure? Well, that is the perfect tape to use when you want to make a recording of yourself playing electric guitar along to *Stairway To Heaven*.

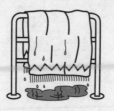

## SOGGY

**!**

A mean spouse will always ensure that their partner's towel is wet, by whatever means necessary. And while you are at it, keep the bathroom floor wet to ensure that your partner's socks are always wet, too.

## SLEEPLESS NIGHTS FOR SOME

Has your partner gone on a health kick that includes giving up coffee? Substitute caffeinated for decaf and have the joy of watching them bounce off the walls.

## NIGHT MOVES

Surprise your partner with a new move in bed. At first they'll be thrilled, but then the paranoia will set in and they'll make themselves sick wondering who you learned it from.

## YES, YOUR ASS DOES LOOK BIG

Next time your wife asks you if the skirt she is wearing makes her look fat, tell her that it's not the skirt that makes her look fat, it's the fat that makes her look fat.

# BURN BABY BURN

There is no quicker and easier way to be mean,
than to flush the toilet while your partner is in
the shower. Laugh and clap as they perform the
"dance of the scalding skin."

## THE BEST THINGS COME IN SMALL BLUE BOXES

Put a small blue box from Tiffany's in a place where your wife will see it. She will spend days anticipating what could be inside. You of course will put a rock inside. A real rock, not a diamond. When she opens it and looks disappointed, explain that it was a rock you found on your first date. She may even pretend to appreciate the sentiment.

## MERCY DASH

Send your husband out for tampons in the middle of the night. When he comes back bedraggled, soaking wet and wild eyed, blithely inform him that you don't actually need them now, but it is always good to have some on hand.

## ARE YOU READY YET?

Going out for a big night and the wife has been getting ready for hours? When she finally emerges all dressed up and with make-up perfectly in place, look her over and proceed to ask when she is going to get ready.

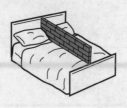

## SEX STING

Tease your husband with the promise of kinky sex, and when he's good and hot tell him you are going to be having a form of Tantric Sex that involves no touching. Tell him he has to will himself to orgasm. See if he can.

## FIGHTING MAD

Didn't have enough time to get to the gym today? Then pick a fight with your partner. The average domestic argument burns off up to 200 calories. You get to make your partner upset and get a really good workout at the same time.

## GUNS 'N' ROSES

Does your husband have a T-shirt that he has been treasuring since he was fifteen because he bought it at his first rock concert? Well, can you think of a better rag to clean the windows with?

## ECONOMIZE

You and your partner going on a vacation? Offer to book the flight. Book yourself into First Class and your partner into Coach. They'll be furious, but they'll be easy to avoid. You can wait in the First Class Lounge, and once on the plane the airline staff will ensure that riffraff from the back of the plane don't bother you.

## CHOP CHOP

If your husband is uncircumcised, it is fun to insist that the time has come for it to happen. Whenever you see him looking relaxed, mime a scissor motion with your fingers. Every so often whisper the words, "Snip, snip." Soon you will have him sweating and crossing his legs at the mere sight of a butter knife.

# BEING OF UNSOUND MIND

When you die, leave some money in your will for a fake lawyer to read out a fake will, in which your spouse will only inherit if they agree never to have another relationship and join a religious order. After the screaming has gone on for long enough (that is, for several years), the fake lawyer can then reveal the truth.

• EX-LOVERS •

X MARKS THE SPOT

## SEXUAL HEALING

•
•
•

Send a fax to your ex's boss detailing all the ways in which they were sexually dysfunctional. Include helpful illustrations. You get extra points if you send a video. If you're lucky it'll make the office Christmas party.

# IF ANYONE HERE HAS ANY OBJECTION...

No ex should be allowed to enjoy their wedding without a visit from you telling all the guests about their shortcomings. Do this even if you aren't actually bitter about the breakup, just for the sheer joy of it.

## HEMMED IN

Everyone knows the trick of breaking into your ex's apartment and putting seafood in their curtain hems and air vents. This is an oldie but a goodie, too, and really does torture them for some time. Don't feel badly about it, they've probably done it to someone else. Maybe you.

## CRY FOR HELP

Starved for attention after you've been dumped?
Phone your ex in the middle of the night
threatening suicide. When they hurry over, act
confused and say you were just calling to tell
them about a television show you were watching.

# SEND A BOUQUET

If your ex is in a new relationship, you simply must send them flowers anonymously, thanking them for everything.

## OH GOD! OH GOD! OH GOD!

Randomly call an ex and tell them that you faked every orgasm (even if you didn't) during your relationship. This should plant a seed of doubt in their minds that could hamper them for the rest of their lives. How cool is that?

CONGRATULATIONS

If you're a woman, call an ex from a few years ago and casually mention that you two have a child together. Tell him you thought he'd like to know. You can tell him the truth eventually, but it should be a good show for a while. You can try this if you're a man, but it may not be as effective.

## OUT YOURSELF

Randomly call an ex and inform them cheerfully that your time with them has turned you gay. Thank them for being so bad in bed that you finally found your true self and sexuality.

## FRIENDS DISUNITED

Go on friendster.com pretending to be your ex. Write a lot of sad, pathetic things about their life. End it with a statement proclaiming themselves a loser and proud of it.

## ALL CLAPPED OUT

Always be prepared in case you run into your ex's new partner. When it finally happens, hand them a dose of penicillin to pass on to your ex, and ask whether the oozing discharge has cleared up yet.

## WHOA, BACK UP

Never leave a relationship without deleting all your ex's "favorites" and shortcuts from their computer. While you're at it, delete their address book file. Oh, and you might as well wipe the whole hard drive while you're sitting there. The backups you made will make admirable hostages for the divorce negotiations.

## IN THE PINK

Before you leave your ex's house for the last time slip a brand new red garment into the washing machine. Odds are, the next wash in that washing machine will be a white wash. Or, as it will henceforth be known, a pink wash.

## DOUBLE-D CUP

Is your ex a woman? Anonymously send her a brochure from a breast enhancement clinic. Include a note that says, "We all joined together to buy you this. Signed, Every Man Who ever Attempted to Locate Your Breasts."

## FLACCID TEST

Is your ex a man? Anonymously send him a bottle of Viagra. Include a note that says, "We all joined together to buy this for you. Signed, Every Woman You Have ever Slept with." If he didn't need it before, he sure will need it now.

WWW.MYEXISCRAPINBED.COM

Did you and your ex videotape the sex? Post it on the Internet. With hope they'll be humiliated. The downside to this is you could make them a star—look what happened with Paris Hilton. So only do this if your ex looks repulsive.

# DON'T WAIT FOR A PROPOSAL

If after five years of living together he still says
he's not the "marrying" kind, see if he's the
"screaming while being stabbed with a fork" kind.

## CHANGE THE LOCKS

Always keep the spare key to your ex's house in case
of emergencies. For instance, a major emergency
is that you were dumped six months ago and you
still feel angry and bitter enough to sneak into
their house and plant your underwear some place
where their new partner will find it.

## A MIXED SALAD

Have you just been dumped and told to vacate the premises? Leave a little present behind. Completely wet the bathmat and sprinkle it with watercress seeds. In a few days, salad will be freely available in your ex's bathroom.

## I'D LIKE TO THANK

Okay, the odds are slim that this will happen, but just in case you ever win an Oscar, do not pass up the opportunity to denigrate your ex in your speech. A simple, "I'd like to thank that rat bastard Ed Cox for being a numbskull" should get your point across to billions of people.

## MY NEW BEST FRIEND

Become good friends with your ex's new partner.
It will freak your ex out.

## HERE'S MY CARD

Feel like sabotaging your ex's business dealings? Why not have some business cards printed up, identical in almost every respect to their existing cards, and secrete them in your ex's cardholder. Clients will be puzzled when handed a card that reads: "John Smith: Incompetent Senior Accountant Executive and Certified Idiot."

## PAPPED OUT

Mock up a photograph on your computer of your ex leaving a famous night club with a celebrity, and send it to a newspaper. It might be fun for your ex to have the world's press camped outside their door for a couple of days until the confusion is cleared up.

# BY THE WAY, I'M RICH

**⋮**

Just after the divorce papers are signed, let slip to your ex that you have just been informed of a distant relative leaving you several millions in their will, and what a pity they won't be able to share any of it. If only they had treated you better and not had that affair.

## DO IT WITH POLISH

As you pack your bags and leave your ex's house for good, be sure to coat all their phones with shoe polish. You get extra points if they use the phone right before they go on their first date.

## GOOD YEAR

⋮

What could be more romantic than renting the Goodyear Blimp to fly over a sporting event flashing a proposal? Nothing. So what could be meaner than hiring the Blimp to say: "Terry. It's over. You're dumped."

## YOUR MOTHER LOVES ME

Always ingratiate yourself with the family of the person you are in a relationship with so you become indispensable. This way, when you get dumped, your ex will get all the blame. They will spend the rest of their life hearing about how wonderful you are and how they'll never do better.

## PINS AND NEEDLES

•
•

Does your ex have an injury or pain? Why not visit their house and plant a voodoo doll that resembles them, with pins in the exact location of these injuries. Imagine their bewilderment as they contemplate the possibilities of black magic.

## HAVE YOU SEEN THIS CAT?

Take photos of your ex's overfriendly cat and print up your own missing posters, promising a huge reward if found. Every time someone sees the poor kitty they'll take him home and annoy your ex for money.

# FIVE O'CLOCK SHADOW

Dump your girlfriend while she is bleaching her moustache. She will not be in any position to argue (because it will dislodge the bleach). Plus it will deepen the shame of her being hairy.

# I'LL MAKE YOU AN OFFER...

If your partner dares to dump you in a callous manner, tell them to watch their back because your cousin Guido will take care of them. The fact that the closest you have to a "connected" cousin is an old aunt in New Jersey should have no bearing on scaring your ex silly.

## WHEN YOU CARE ENOUGH TO
## SEND THE VERY BEST

Be a thoughtful ex. Always send birthday cards,
Christmas presents, Valentines chocolates, May
Day flowers, first day of summer thoughts, Labor
Day Greetings, Solstice Salutations... In fact,
just contact them every day. Don't let the fact
that they have a new partner or an old
restraining order get in your way.

# GUESS WHO'S COMING TO DINNER?

Let bygones be bygones. Have a dinner party and invite your ex. Of course all the other dinner guests should be an ex of your ex.

# USE YOUR HEAD AND SHOULDERS

As you leave your ex's house for the last time, be sure to glue the tops of their shampoo and shower gel bottles shut. Sure hope they don't get a hernia trying to open them...

## HELLO. DO YOU LOVE ME?

Call someone who was devastated when you dumped them just to see if they still love you. They do? Good. Just checking.

# REVENGE IS SWEET

If you got dumped because you let yourself go, being mean becomes easy. Lose lots of weight, get a great haircut and a tan, buy a sexy wardrobe, then run into your ex "accidentally." How mean is that?

• AND FINALLY... •

## WHERE THERE'S A WILL

!

Spend your life amassing a huge fortune. Do nothing but make money. Don't marry or have children. Promise everyone you know that you're going to leave all your money to them. But really leave all your money to some obscure animal charity. Imagine everyone's disappointment at the reading of the will. Who's laughing now?